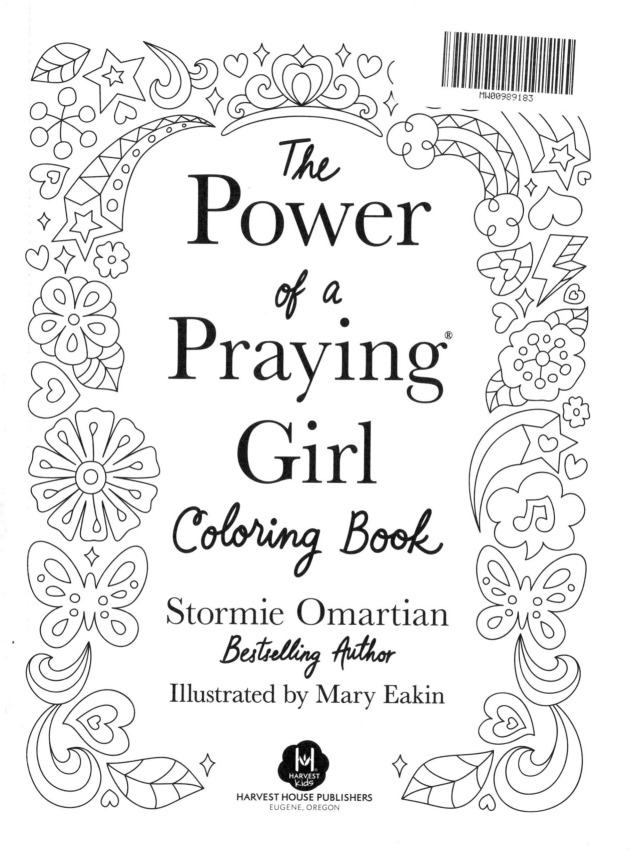

The Power of a Praying Girl

Coloring Book

Stormie Omartian
Bestselling Author

Illustrated by Mary Eakin

HARVEST Kids

HARVEST HOUSE PUBLISHERS
EUGENE, OREGON

Scripture quotations are taken from the New King James Version®. Copyright © 1982 by Thomas Nelson, Inc. Used by permission. All rights reserved.

Cover and interior illustration and design by Mary Eakin

For bulk, special sales, or ministry purchases, please call 1 (800) 547-8979.
Email: Customerservice@hhpbooks.com

This logo is a federally registered trademark of the Hawkins Children's LLC. Harvest House Publishers, Inc., is the exclusive licensee of this trademark.

THE POWER OF A PRAYING is a trademark of the Hawkins Children's LLC. Harvest House Publishers, Inc., is the exclusive licensee of the trademark THE POWER OF A PRAYING.

The Power of a Praying® Girl Coloring Book
Text copyright © 2022 by Stormie Omartian
Artwork © 2022 by Mary Eakin
Published by Harvest House Publishers
Eugene, Oregon 97408
www.harvesthousepublishers.com

ISBN 978-0-7369-8373-0 (pbk.)

Printed in the United States of America

22 23 24 25 26 27 28 29 30 / VP / 10 9 8 7 6 5 4 3 2 1

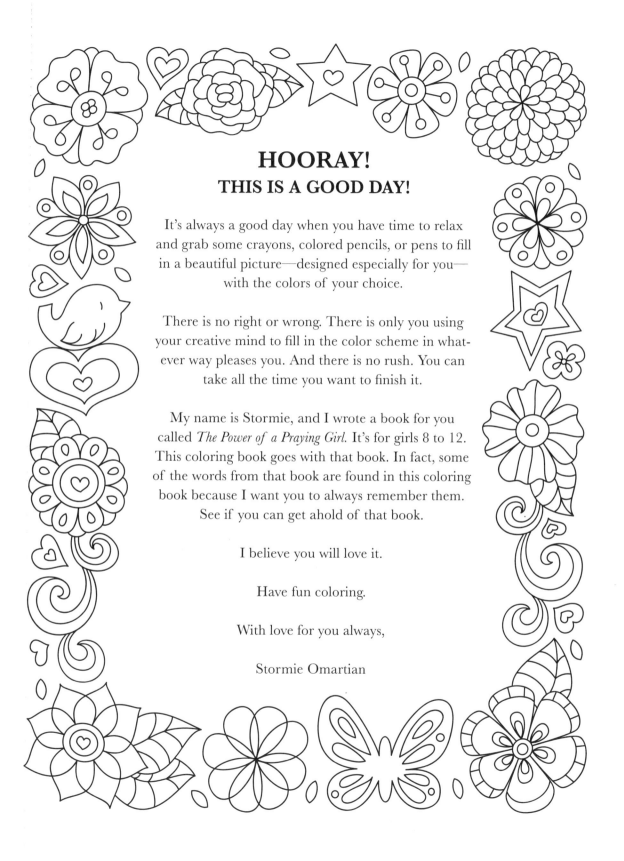

HOORAY!
THIS IS A GOOD DAY!

It's always a good day when you have time to relax and grab some crayons, colored pencils, or pens to fill in a beautiful picture—designed especially for you— with the colors of your choice.

There is no right or wrong. There is only you using your creative mind to fill in the color scheme in whatever way pleases you. And there is no rush. You can take all the time you want to finish it.

My name is Stormie, and I wrote a book for you called *The Power of a Praying Girl*. It's for girls 8 to 12. This coloring book goes with that book. In fact, some of the words from that book are found in this coloring book because I want you to always remember them. See if you can get ahold of that book.

I believe you will love it.

Have fun coloring.

With love for you always,

Stormie Omartian

Lord, help me to be loving, kind, helpful, happy, and thankful.

He will direct my paths.

(see Proverbs 3:6)

Lord, I want to spend quiet time with you.

God has great plans for me because He loves me.

(see Jeremiah 29:11)

Nothing is too hard for God.

Lord, lead me in everything I do.

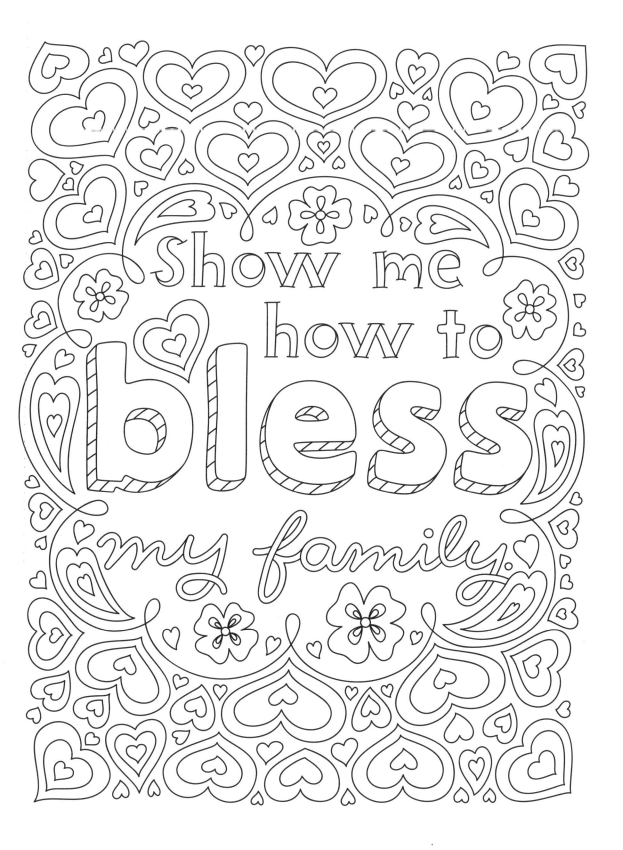

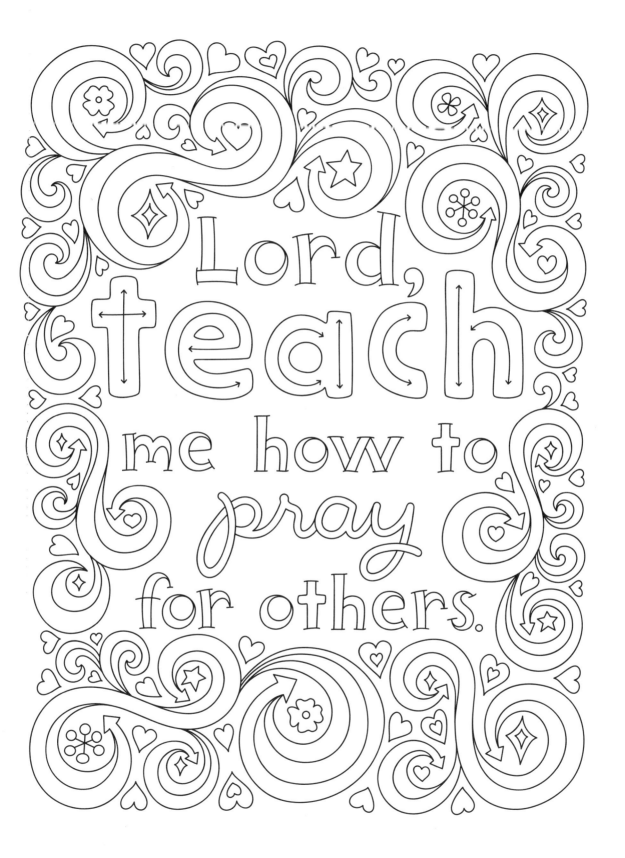

Help me to always honor my father and mother.

God wants to teach me how to live His way.

Heavenly Father, help me to wait patiently for the answer to my prayers.

Lord, help me to trust You whenever I pray.

Stormie Omartian is the bestselling author of the Power of a Praying® series, which includes *The Power of a Praying® Teen*. Her other books include *A Book of Prayers for Young Women* and *Just Enough Light for the Step I'm On*. (More than 40 million copies of her books have been sold worldwide.) Stormie and her husband, Michael, have been married more than 48 years. They are the parents of two married children and have two granddaughters. www.stormieomartian.com

Mary Eakin is a graduate of the Academy of Art University of San Francisco and was an award-winning graphic designer for Hallmark's gift book division for nine years. She's also the author of *Mind Delights* and *Brain Snacks*. Mary lives with her husband and two children in Maryland. www.maryeakin.com

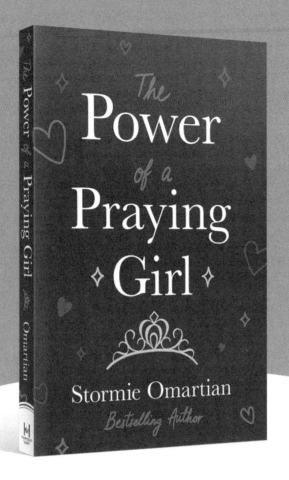